Sermon Series

poems by

Stephanie Harper

Finishing Line Press
Georgetown, Kentucky

Sermon Series

Copyright © 2017 by Stephanie Harper
ISBN 978-1-63534-301-4 First Edition
All rights reserved under International and Pan-American Copyright Conventions.
No part of this book may be reproduced in any manner whatsoever without written permission from the publisher, except in the case of brief quotations embodied in critical articles and reviews.

ACKNOWLEDGMENTS

The poems in this collection were all directly inspired by sermons and worship experiences at Abiding Hope Church in Littleton, Colorado. While the poems in this collection are meant to be universally spiritual in nature and do not conspire to adhere to a particular religious tradition, they are thematically arranged to pay homage to the Lutheran liturgical calendar, beginning with the season of Advent.

Publisher: Leah Maines

Editor: Christen Kincaid

Cover Art: Kyle Colby of KColby Photography

Author Photo: Kyle Colby of KColby Photography

Cover Design: Elizabeth Maines McCleavy

Printed in the USA on acid-free paper.
Order online: www.finishinglinepress.com
            also available on amazon.com

Author inquiries and mail orders:
Finishing Line Press
P. O. Box 1626
Georgetown, Kentucky 40324
U. S. A.

Table of Contents

Expectation

Expectation 1
Gray 2
Magnify 3
Waiting 4
How to Pray 5
Thousands of Stars 6
Goodness 7
Meaning 8
Messengers 9
Breathing 10
Gift of Light 11
Worship 12

Epiphanies

Epiphanies 15
Death Waits 16
Star Stuff 17
Drifting 18
Darkness 19
Aspens 20
Small Word 21
Abundance 22
Heckling 23
Heartbeat 24
This Joy 25
Meadow 26
Cosmos 27
Mid-Air 28
Wounds 29
Systems 30
Stones 31
Justice 32
Dying 33
The Moth 34

Recognition 35
Burial Ground 36
Blessing 37
Synapses 38
Floodwater 39
Shrubs 40
Peace be With You 41
Home 42
What We Are 43

Expression

Expression 47
Field of Desire 48
Reconcile 49
Night Sky 50
Small Prophet 51
Bread of Life 52
The Deer 53
Your Freedom 54
Scarcity 55
Water and Words 56
Low 57
Sin 58
Hunger 59
Disturbance 60
Spirits 61
The Seed 62
Hardening 63
Encounter 64
The Beach 65
Language 66
Remaking 67
Dandelion 68
Proof 69
Grace 70
Story 71
Apple 72
Kingdom Come 73

To Doug, Chad, Glenn, Laura, Robin, Joel and the entire Abiding Hope community for challenging and inspiring.

Expectation

Expectation

I am waiting for the flame
of an aged wax candle,
the expectation of light—
an arrival.

Gray

Particles blend together
in an artful sort of way
like colors in a painter's hand.

This is where I choose
to dwell.

This gray place
is where I will make my stand.

Magnify

How do we magnify
what's beyond seeing?

The soul.
The mystery.

Or how you and I
are steeped in the cover

of a kind of love
so much deeper

then knowing
or understanding,

feeling beyond feeling,
that is both all the noise

and the silence.

How do we magnify
a world so far beyond our own?

Waiting

I know something of waiting;
of the clock ticking
standstill,
the loneliness
of not knowing
what I am seeking.

I know this waiting—
or perhaps longing
is a better word.

I know the weight
of this aching.

No answers,
only questions upon questions
in my head.

How to Pray

How can you expect to drop
to your knees
with your heart beating
violently
in your chest?

I know this anger comes so easily.

How difficult it is
to say to yourself,
"Do not be afraid."

And yet,
how will you fall
to your knees and pray
if it isn't love
on your lips?

How will you empty yourself?

Thousands of Stars

I crave the sunlight,
the heat like a whispered answer
to some important question,
but also the darkness,

the dead of night,
where the sky bursts open with
the spark of a thousand stars
that shine like signal fires.

Those lights so far away
they drown in the morning sun,
can guide my lost heart
in a kind of direction.

Goodness

Good news comes
in a humble presentation,
like a feather,
so light and taken
wherever the wind blows
as though this is exactly
where it is meant to be.

This is how goodness
enters the heart,
so faint,
a whisper.

This is where good things
take root
like a freshly sprouted tree
as it slowly pokes it's way
to the surface.

The good in this world
comes steady,
like a stream,
as alive and unnoticed
as gravity.

Meaning

I want to be alive
in the simplicity of what it means
to exhale a slow breath
so heavy I can see it
against the glass in the cold
of the stiff morning air.

Messengers

I have seen messengers in this world.

I have seen them
in the particles of dust
that float in a ray of sun
streaming through the window
as though time itself
has suspended.

I have seen them
in drops of water
hanging from the icicles
at the corner of my roof
as though put there
to bring water to the earth.

I have seen these messengers
and I know something of wonder
and of joy.

Breathing

The world waits
in my inhalation
and I am in
and of it.

You see,
this is the secret
of breathing.

Gift of Light

I want to be a gift to this world.

I want to hold a light in my hands,
palms upturned and shaking.

This is no small thing,
I know.

Sometimes I want to take this light
and hide it.

Sometimes the light dims
in the hollows beneath my ribs.

How then can I give it?

This trying, I think, in spite of myself,
is sufficient.

Worship

The flower opens
to the morning sun,
unfolding,
and I think
our definition of worship
is not enough.

It is too small,
too narrow,
like a crack in the wall
or a sliver of glass,
just a small portion
of a shattered whole.

But this world
is a sacred place
and this living
is what it means to worship
every second,
each new day.

Epiphanies

Epiphanies

Some epiphanies come
like a burning, bright light
so hot that when you shut your eyes,
you see the shadows dancing.

I've spent too much time
waiting for that photographic flash.

I'll let a sense of revelation glide by
shrouded in a gray-black cloud,
dense with the tracks that have led me
blinking through the smoke.

Though reddened and watery,
I will let my eyes burn.

Death Waits

Death waits

in the shadows that cling
to the corners of your smile,

the darkness that lurks
in the lines of your face,

when you say you still remember
what it means to be alive.

I've tasted the shade
on the spot above your lip,

smelled the rot
on the surface of your skin.

You're decaying in the way
all dead things decay,

alone in your own quiet space.

Star Stuff

"We are star-stuff"
      -says Sagan,
who should probably
know. But maybe
there's more than
2% heavy elements
in the human soul.

Drifting

I've been drifting
in a wooden boat

carved by my
own hands

so long
I've forgotten

what it is
to stand

on the shore or
feel the sand

as it clings
to my feet,

weightless
against the bottoms.

Darkness

You fear the outer darkness,
the dying of the light,
but what of the murkiness
between your ribs,
thick as sludge.

The darkness that
creeps into the spaces
between your words,
the quiet cadence
of what you cannot
bring yourself to say.

This darkness
settles over you
like a dense cloud,
smoke and ash,
where your fire
has gone out.

Aspens

I mourn for the
barren branches of
a patch of aspens
stark in the winter cold.

Overwhelmed,
I stand
in the presence
of such nakedness,

like arms and legs,
bodies stripped of
some living and
essential part.

But these trees
know their place
here in the grove
and they rise,

waiting for a splinter
of sunlight
in and amidst
the snow.

Small World

We harness
the generosities of the earth
as though the ground is ours
for the taking.

This world is vast and incomprehensible.

How can we think
we somehow rise above it,
when our feet are
firmly planted in the dirt?

We are such a small part of it all.

Abundance

I am interested
in the kind of love
that overwhelms in the
painful warmth of sacrifice,
so my skin pricks
when I think of suffering,
the kind that dries the insides,
and sometimes all I can do
is reach out and share
a glass of water,
offer the last drop,
and hope for abundance.

Heckling

Afternoon in the winter sun,
and I walk as thoughts whirl inside me
and I am not lost in the peace of the ice
as it cracks in the unusual January heat.

I am not aware of the gift of this warmth.

Then I hear the swell of the geese
afloat at the melted center of the lake
a rising cry as they begin to stir,
to open their wings and rise.

And I am not in my own mind anymore.

I am here on a concrete path
putting one foot in front of the other,
brought to the present by a
grouping of black dots in the sky.

In this heckling, I am reminded.

Heartbeat

I cannot always track the pace
of my own heart beating.

I get lost in the pounding
of whispered drums
against my ribs.

Those vibrations stick like mud
and my body aches with the cracking.

I need to hear the steady throb,
a snapping of branches—
as it pumps

and every inhalation expands with awe.

This Joy

I long for the capacity
to open my heart to
a great joy,
like the flowers
open to the morning light,
the leaves extend green,
growing with the
weight of water.

I long for this joy,
not simple,
not artificial,
but as natural as
streaks of orange
paint the dawn sky.

Meadow

When you find
yourself
in an open meadow
lay down
so the high grass
scratches your arms
resting out and open,
palms up,
greeting the vastness
of sky—
you have opened
your vulnerable heart
to drink the light.

Feel the heat
as your face flushes
and your hands and feet
swell
with the warmth
of the sun—
let your skin
dampen,
let the day
tickle the skin
of your throat
as you breathe,
so sure, so deep.

Cosmos

Does humanity exist
in the order of the cosmos?

Immense and mathematical,
what I see when I look

up at an obscure night sky,
so dark and clear

I feel I could almost
reach out and capture

the milky light
in the palm of my hand.

We are the remnants
of collapsed stars.

Ours is the cycle
of the universe.

Mid-Air

I exist in mid-air.

I will hit the earth
like a rock hard clump of dust
and leave a crater in my wake.

I will hit the dirt
as though it were a drum
and I'm a purposeful rhythm

beating.

Wounds

You conceal your wounds,
the scars and open sores,
in a thin cloth,
just enough to hide them.

This is a mistake.

These wounds,
leave them uncovered,
they reflect a soft and subtle light,
a lesson.

Systems

I exist in systems,
knitted together,
threads from old stories.

These systems rest
in layers like maps,
a human topography.

I haven't found a system
for freedom,
for breathing.

I haven't found a way
to make peace with dark matter,
the spaces between the cracks.

But every morning
I am awake
and learning.

Stones

You are a mythology of stones.

I've seen the way they've filled
your valleys,
washed by the creeks formed
in the bends of your limbs.

These rocks—some jagged, some smooth as bone—
perhaps they aren't an added weight,
but a part of you,
pieces breaking free from the foundation.

You could bury them deep in the dirt
or roll them away,
expose the splendor
at the heart of you.

Justice

Justice is not a house
of your own making.

You cannot assemble it
from your arsenal of sticks.

You cannot speak the words
and open a locked door.

Don't waste yourself on "can't."
Don't hide in a windowless room.

Trust your whole self to the only justice—love.

Dying

This dying
is not a stoppage
of breath.

Only an exhalation.

This is the kind of death
that empties you for
another existence.

The Moth

You cannot catch a gypsy moth
beneath a small, glass jar
and expect that she will live.

You drop a few leaves,
perhaps a purple flower,
poke holes in the metal for breathing.

She might flutter at first,
come to the top and cling
in the desperation of perceived freedom
but she will settle.

She will stay grounded until her end.

You cannot trap certain lively things
and expect them to remain
there for your viewing.

You have to give the wild
room to breathe.

Recognition

You seek your great reward
or at least an acknowledgement.

You crave the sound of your name
on someone's lips,
in praise, in adoration.

You seek to be remembered.

But, tell me,
are you awarded for breathing?

Why then,
must you seek acknowledgement
for living?

This should be recognition enough.

Burial Ground

My body is a burial ground
caked in regret,
sacred and undiscovered.

This earth's been left unturned,
hallowed and waiting,
and I am ready to make myself again.

Blessing

Blessed are you—
the one who stumbles.

You have been shown
how to turn your heart
toward love.

You understand
the reasons why
you must be broken
over and over again.

Synapses

I tread
the water of words
and thoughts blossom
into trees
of dialogue.

They grow
higher and wider
and senses
have occasion
to bud.

These ideas
fire with
an electric spark
and my eyes
alight with wonder.

Floodwater

This is the struggle
that surges within me
like a slow rising river,
and even though I stand
on the bank
piling bags of sand
against the truth of it,
eventually the water
comes over the edge,
and I am immersed
in my own significance.

Shrubs

In my heart
you planted a seed.

I thought
you had given me a tree
but it grew outward,
the twigs spread wide.

This was the gift you gave me—
not branches, but shrubs.

Peace Be With You

Peace be with you
in the quiet of a steady
rising dawn,
when the day has
barely opened.

Peace be with you
in the warmth
of a noon sun
as it beats down
and burns.

Peace be with you
in the twilight glow,
the dusk settling
heavy,
like fog.

Peace be with you
in the night when no stars
alight the sky
and the moon
stays hidden.

This peace be with you
always,
in the constancy of now.

Home

I am shaken.
I am off center and wandering.
I am here in the dirt
and somehow the pulsing
at my throat,
a beating,
feels like a home
of it's own.

What We Are

We are all water.
We are cells and skin and vapor.
We are the earth, the sky,
the heat at the center,
and the cold in faraway reaches,
the ones that lie in darkness.
We are made of stars.

Expression

Expression

I will find the path to express this joy,
the joy in my body,
the joy that moves through blood and bone.

I will not hold it close to my heart,
like some secret treasure that needs protecting.

I will not let this joy wither.

I will not let it waste away,
a budding green plant stripped of it's source of water.

I will let it open out of me like the petals of a rose.

I will exhale this joy as though it were air.

Field of Desire

For Rumi

My desires reside in a field of wheat and weeds.

The ones I should harvest
and those I should leave behind,
pull up, bundle together, and burn.

I cannot separate them,
the roots have intertwined—
pulling the one will only destroy the other.

Desires grow together and cannot be undone.

Reconcile

Look closely and you will see two worlds.

One bears down on you
with the weight of boulders.

The other waits in the quiet corners
inside of you, collecting dust.

On occasion, it reaches out
to take your sadness in its arms.

Speak the words that reconcile.
Two worlds want to be one.

Night Sky

If I asked you to paint
a vivid picture of your loneliness,
it would be moonlight.

You inhabit the electric
spark of purple night,
the vastness of an open sky.

I see it in the way your eyes
settle in that distant place,
the one just above my shoulder.

You've spent your time not sleeping,
laying on your back in cold grass,
staring up at the endlessness.

But where you see
your own inevitable smallness,
I see possibility—infinite.

Small Prophet

For Maya

I believe this child is a prophet.

I believe this small person
so fragile,
brittle as a dried leaf,
this child
changes everything.

This child can teach
so much of love
in the joy of a laugh,
high-pitched and gurgling,
or the stark sound of a cry,
tears flowing with freedom.

This child can remind us
of our own hearts beating.

Bread of Life

I should imagine this spongy square,
a little underdone,
like mush,
not as a blend of flour
but of flesh.

This is a hard thing to ask.

To take a piece in my mouth,
between my back teeth,
chewing as I think,
"this is the body,
the skin."

I am not an eater of men,
of Messiahs,
and this wheat-flesh
only reminds me
of my downfalls.

I am not imaginative enough
to transfigure this piece
in the palm
of my hand—
I see only bread.

Yet, even in this,
I believe there is something,
in the taking and the breaking,
a reminder that this is a place
of freedom.

The Deer

Does the deer fear the shadows of the forest?

It cannot know what waits,
what gnashing thing might befall it.

Does it cower?

No, this deer continues
to graze on green grass
until the crack of a branch
under some secret foot
signals danger.

I long to go about my own life
no matter the shadows.
I long to wander through the darkness
like the deer.

Your Freedom

You will not fight
a great attendance of freedom
alone on an open road.

This solitude,
the dirt beneath your feet,
brings focus, even peace,
the way you set yourself on a path
and carry the weight on your shoulders,
a sign of your own strength.

But freedom so precious,
an uninhibited grace,
can only be found
in the center of a place
created in a relationship of love,
one with you and the rest of the world.

Scarcity

I've fallen into a trap of scarcity,
where nothing is enough.

Shame on me.

I've forgotten the rich soil of the earth,
the air I breathe,
how I am of this world,
how I am everything.

If I lay down in the grass and look up
at an uncertain sky, smell the coming rain,
I can almost reverse it.

Water and Words

This is about water,
and also words,
because I've seen them drip
from your mouth in steady streams
where they fall to the ground
and absorb the sound
of the air as it flows
between shadows—

the ones that whisper,
"Don't wait.
Just go."

Low

On the cold earth,
where I've fallen to my knees,
laid my body flat
so the side of my face
presses into the dirt,
on this spot,
so broken,
here I encounter the grace
only discovered
in the lowest places,
the grace that washes over
my tired body,
pushes me upward
to stand,
unsteady,
on my feet again.

Sin

Our great sin is not misdeed
but contamination,
like the toxic sludge
of the Animas River,
carried through the water
to poison all tributaries,
a web a veins,
strings of connection,
this is how we sin.

This is how we lose sight
of who we are,
who we can be,
forgetting the cool waters
of our purpose
to flow with gratitude,
hands clasped together in prayer.

Hunger

On a cool morning I wake.

I feel a twisting,
a turning,
pulling of taffy,
as though my stomach
rolls up and in on itself
and I know the time
to end this hunger
is now.

I may take out the milk,
a bowl of cereal,
but this is never enough,
not for this feeling,
the heaving emptiness
in the pit
of me.

I need more.
Perhaps love.
Perhaps the sun.
Perhaps gratitude
for a new morning.

I will drive this hunger
out with the dawn.

Disturbance

I seek the calm
of a dark evening
with the moon a silver light,
a sliver in the sky.

I find great peace in
setting myself somewhere
amidst the near silence—
I crave this.

Still, sometimes
I need the quiet broken:
a crack of a branch
or the rustle of leaves.

Sometimes I need to remember
that there exists a world
much greater then
me.

Spirits

I sometimes struggle to believe
that spirits inhabit us all—
  Even though I see
  the greening of the earth
  in the aftermath of rain,
  even though I feel
  the electric twinge
  of something beneath
  the surface of my skin,
  even though I've known
  both sorrow and joy
  so deep I feel a chasm
  within me
  as it opens and fills
  over and over again.
I struggle to believe in this steadfast
yet ephemeral love that resonates
within and against the sinews of everything.

The Seed

You planted a seed
at the center of me,
nurtured it with water,
with breath.

In the hot, damp hollows
more a cavern then a well,
this seed of yours
took root.

I didn't know
what great, green thing
would sprout,
grip me and entwine
with my limbs.

Sometimes the knots constricted.

Still,
I trusted that you had planted
something that mattered
more than myself.

Hardening

Keep me far away
from the hardening of a heart
like freshly poured cement.

This life is difficult,
I know.

I have felt the rocky surface of this world,
the brick and the stone,
and it has stopped me,
left me breathless
as the crack of a freshly broken bone.

Still, I wish to remain soft,
like the fresh pine just under the bark,
peeled back and exposed.

Encounter

How do you encounter
the secret spaces of this living?

How do you seek
what you cannot confirm?

How do you touch
what pulses just beneath the current
of softly moving air?

I do not know the answer.

I have sought
but never found
these unknowable things.

Still,
I feel a presence.

Still, I know I've encountered something,
perhaps a door.

The Beach

We think we own the sun
as we lay on a sand beach,
beads of perspiration on
reddening skin.

We can almost believe
these rays manifested for us,
and we lap them up as though
the day owes us this light.

We are so small.
This moment is a gift
and we are just beginning
to taste it.

Language

I do not understand this language of freedom.

My tongue twists
over the words beyond words,
the ones that bubble up from within
some secret place in the earth,
or that shine in the light of the dawn
illuming particles of dust
that brush the skin of my arms
and set my hair standing.

I do not know what it is to be free
in a true and unencumbered way.

I cannot utter those sacred, babbling phrases,
because I haven't the capacity to translate.

And yet, in my breath, I feel this language
is already a part of me.

Remaking

Can you remake a broken vessel,
one dropped and shattered against the floor,
in pieces, so many, so numerous,
dotting the ground like gravel or stars?

If you pick up all the small parts
and arrange them back together
section by section,
can you mend the brokenness
into the same thing it was
in the beginning?

Can you make this vessel whole?
I believe you can make it something
if not entirely unchanged,
at least repaired.

Dandelion

Consider the abandon
of the dandelion seed,
the way it falls wherever
the breeze disperses.

It may catch
on my eyelashes,
tickle the skin of my cheek
until I flick it away.

The seed does not fear
the unknown of where
it might end:
it goes where it has to.

Proof

If you need proof
that light shines
in the quiet moments
of every day,
you need only to
rest your hand
on that place
at the center
of your chest.

There is a refuge
in the rhythm,
in the rise and fall
of your shoulders
as you breathe
out and in,
like the steady tide
as it moves
across the sand.

This is a place
you can stay
for a while.
This is a place
you can rest.
This is a place
where you feel
in your body
an invocation.

Grace

Grace is a rooted mystery,
one I've searched for
in the darkened corners
of a walled-in structure
of my own making.

In this space I ask
"What am I doing here now?"

The fact that I have
to step outside,
feel the cold earth
on the soles of my feet,
is itself a kind of answer.

This is grace,
here where I never thought
to find it.

Story

You are your own story,
so am I.

I believe we both tell the truth in this,
no matter the differences,
the ones of who we are and
where we will be going.

It seems we can have two truths
or more
and neither one of us is wrong.

So let our stories intertwine
like the reeds of a basket,
woven together to hold us both.

Apple

A fall apple
smooth in my palms,
so crisp between my teeth.

The apple grows
only to be harvested,
to be eaten.

If only I could fathom
this sense of purpose.

If only I could serve
so purely,
so incidentally.

If only my skin grew
ripe and red.

Kingdom Come

I will let this kingdom come
not with gold and glory,
for white horses should remain
unbridled.

I will let it come
with quiet purpose,
the way a steady stream
glides
over smoothly faceted stone.

Stephanie Harper received her Bachelor's in English from the University of Colorado in 2009. She went on to complete her Master's of Fine Arts in Creative Writing from Fairfield University in 2012. Her fiction, nonfiction, and poetry can be found in *The Huffington Post, HelloGiggles, HerStories, The Montreal Review, Poetry Quarterly, Midwest Literary Magazine, Haiku Journal,* and *Spry Literary Journal.* She currently lives in Denver, Colorado.

www.ingramcontent.com/pod-product-compliance
Lightning Source LLC
Chambersburg PA
CBHW070550090426
42735CB00013B/3132